TV and MOVIE TIE-INS

STAR WARS

by James A. Lely

Published by Creative Education, 123 South Broad Street, Mankato, Minnesota 56001.

Cover Photo: Photo Trends

Library of Congress Number: 79-52894   ISBN: 0-87191-700-9

Delight

"The reason that I'm making *Star Wars* is that I want to give young people some sort of faraway, exotic environment for their imagination to run around in. I have a strong feeling about interesting kids in space exploration. I want them to want it."

Star Wars is the dream-come-true of George Lucas, the young writer and director. He wanted to create a movie full of fun. He wanted to create a fantasy movie with the same spirit as Saturday morning cartoons. To accomplish this, he wrote the now-famous story of a young hero, Luke Skywalker, who bravely goes forth to save a galaxy. George Lucas especially likes the character, Luke Skywalker, for he wrote the part to represent himself.

Mark Hamill
as Luke Skywalker

In 1970, when George Lucas was 25, he released his first full-length movie, *THX 1138*. In 1973, he directed the successful *American Graffiti*, a story about Lucas's own youth.

Lucas took his *Star Wars* script to United Artists and Universal Studios, but both rejected it. Twentieth Century-Fox, however, accepted the script and gave Lucas the money to complete work on the story. Lucas wrote the original script differently from the one which was finally used. At first, Lucas didn't want to have any human characters in the film. In his early scripts, he focused on the adventures of See Threepio (C3PO) and Artoo Detoo (R2D2). However, Lucas's friends persuaded him to change the script because they felt no one wants to see a movie about two robots. In this case, they might have been wrong.

As the whole world knows, George Lucas presented his dreams in an extraordinary package. He filled the movie with realistic visions of the future and packed it with adventure. During the last year of production, Lucas worked 361 days, 16 hours a day.

He finally had to release *Star Wars*, but he would have been glad to work on it for another year. George Lucas is a perfectionist.

Roughly 100 million fans have seen *Star Wars* at least once. So far, they've spent $267 million to see it—and that doesn't count popcorn. When *Star Wars* had its first rerun in 1978, it brought in $70 million. As expected, *Star Wars* has been seen by more people and has made more money than any other film.

The movie wasn't cheap: it cost $100,000 a day to produce, for a total of $9 million. But the rewards were great. The film made millionaires out of the three lead actors—Mark Hamill, Harrison Ford, and Carrie Fisher. Eleven sequels are planned, the first to be called *The Empire Strikes Back*. Hamill, Ford, and Fisher, as well as other of the actors, are committed to a three-picture contract. Sir Alec Guinness, who played Obi-Wan Kenobi, will not appear again, but his voice will be heard in the first sequel.

George Lucas will turn the directorship of the first sequel over to Irvin Kersner. The plot for this

Star Wars has been seen by more people and has made more money than any other film.

sequel concerns the Imperial Empire's fight to regain its power.

Toys and other merchandise based on _Star Wars_ characters have grossed well over $200 million so far. Kenner alone is responsible for $60 million in _Star Wars_ toys and dolls. Several books have been published to fill the demand for more information on the movie. These include a book of blueprints of the actual sets, a sketch book, a punch-out book, a _Star Wars_ story book, and a _Star Wars_ calendar.

The movie has been successfully imitated by the new television series _Battlestar Galactica_. John Dykstra, the man who created the brilliant special effects for _Star Wars_, has also created the effects for _Battlestar_. Other films, including _Star Trek_, are being made now to take advantage of the huge interest in science fiction.

Lucas selected an interesting cast for *Star Wars*. The best-known of the actors is Sir Alec Guinness, who has entertained movie fans for the last 44 years. He has performed in many plays and TV shows. He is also well known for his parts in such movies as *The Bridge Over the River Kwai, Lawrence of Arabia, Murder by Death,* and *Dr. Zhivago.* Mark Hamill, who played Luke Skywalker, Harrison Ford as the pilot Han Solo, and Carrie Fisher as Princess Leia became close friends during the filming of *Star Wars. Star Wars* is the first screen role for Carrie Fisher, who is the 21-year-old daughter of singer Eddie Fisher and actress Debbie Reynolds. Critics say she has the finest singing voice in the family. Carrie Fisher lives alone in an apartment on New York's Central Park West. At present, the 5-foot, 1-inch, 99 pound actress takes private acting lessons. Ms. Fisher never finished high school, and claims that she still feels "like a little leaguer at the World Series."

Harrison Ford lives in a quiet, rented home in West Hollywood close to his wife, from whom he is separated, and his children. Before he became a successful actor, he worked as a carpenter.

Alec Guinness
as Ben Kenobi

Photo Credit: 20th Century-Fox Film Corp.

He built a $100,000 studio for Sergio Mendez. He never graduated from college, but it hasn't hurt his career.

His television appearances include *The FBI*, *The Virginian*, and *Gunsmoke*. He also starred in the movie, *Heroes*, with Henry Winkler. Currently, he is appearing in *Force Ten from Navarone* with Robert Shaw and waiting for the next episode of *Star Wars* to begin.

Mark Hamill, 26, had a near-fatal accident early in 1977, just after finishing *Star Wars*. He drove his car over a cliff and needed three operations to repair damages to his face. His nose has been completely rebuilt through plastic surgery. He was depressed after the accident but his friends encouraged him to return to work.

Mark Hamill lives north of Malibu in California. He has been described as a beach bum who likes to play Monopoly and bake cakes. His good looks make him popular with his fans, who have enjoyed him in the movies, *Big Red One* and *Corvette Summer*.

While growing up, Mark lived in ten cities including Yokohama in Japan. He enrolled in Los Angeles City College to avoid the draft. Then he quit at the end of his second year on the day that he received a deferment.

His career includes 89 guest appearances on prime-time TV and a short run in *General Hospital*. With the release of *Star Wars*, he spent a great deal of time doing publicity shots and guest appearances all across the country. Recently he finished a movie called *Stingray*.

George Lucas pulled off the triumph of *Star Wars* with a careful combination of talented actors, incredible special effects, great attention to detail, and an excellent script. The story is drawn from many old science fiction films as well as from Lucas's imagination. His "faraway, exotic environment" has become a second home to millions of fans.

The story is drawn from many old science fiction films...

Dreams

Star Wars starts with a fight in space. An Imperial Cruiser has opened fire on a Rebel Alliance ship and disabled it.

The Alliance to Restore the Republic is the full name of the Rebel Alliance. It had been formed in the Alderaan star system when the Imperial Empire destroyed the Old Republic. The Rebel Alliance's goal is to bring back the Old Republic and smash the evil Imperial Empire.

The Rebel ship which has been hit by the Imperial Cruiser is carrying Princess Leia Organa, the youngest member of the Imperial Senate and the secret leader of the Alliance to Restore the Republic. She is bringing to Alderaan tapes describing the Imperial Empire's new Death

Star—the deadliest weapon yet invented. The Death Star has the ability to blow up an entire planet. Princess Leia's mission is to have the Alderaan scientists find a weakness in the Death Star's defenses so that the Rebels can destroy it.

When the fighting starts, Princess Leia gives the tapes to a robot named Artoo Detoo. Artoo Detoo snares his buddy, See Threepio, and the odd couple jump into an escape pod and eject themselves from the ship. Their destination is the desert planet, Tatooine.

Carrie Fisher
as Princess Leia
with Artoo-Detoo

Photo Credit: 20th Century Fox Film Corp.

Meanwhile, back on the Rebel ship, a mysterious and horrible man dressed in black storms at his troops, demanding that they find the missing tapes. Darth Vader is the Dark Lord of Sith and his anger always terrifies everyone around him. The troops quickly search the ship and find the Princess.

Princess Leia plays innocent, but Darth Vader sees through her act and tells her that he knows that she is a Rebel. When he finds out that a pod has ejected from the ship, he knows that Princess Leia has outsmarted him for the moment. He sends troops after the pod and arrests the Princess.

George Lucas may have been remembering the heroic comic strip figure, Buck Rogers, when he created the young farmer, Luke Skywalker. Luke is just an ordinary youth waiting to go off to college when a strange twist of fate sends him skyrocketing to adventure.

Luke Skywalker is an orphan. Unknown to him, his father was one of the greatest of the Jedi knights. The Jedi knights defended the Old

Republic but were forced to retreat before the Imperial Empire. Luke's father was killed by Darth Vader, a Jedi knight turned bad.

Uncle Owen and Aunt Beru raised Luke Skywalker to be a farmer on Tatooine. They didn't want him to find out about his father's career and perhaps follow in his footsteps.

When the local junk and machine sellers, called the Jawas, drop by Uncle Owen's farm, all they have to offer are a couple of rusty R2 units, some ancient and worthless scrap metal, and a familiar unit called C3PO. This unit is just what Uncle Owen is looking for, so he buys it along with an R2 unit which blows a gasket right away. Conveniently, there is one other R2 unit available. Its name is R2D2. Luke starts cleaning up the new droids and accidentally learns that Artoo Detoo has a secret. The secret is a projected image on a tape of a young woman asking for help from someone named Obi-Wan Kenobi. The name reminds Luke of a man named Ben Kenobi who lives nearby, but his Uncle doesn't think it is the same man. Of course, it is.

Lucas's stage is now completely set...the hero...has made his entrance.

Lucas's stage is now completely set. The hero of the story has made his entrance and has been swept up in the plot to destroy the Death Star. Any doubts Luke might have had about his role in the rebellion disappear when he discovers the brutal murders of his aunt and uncle by the Imperial troopers.

Obi-Wan Kenobi agrees to come out of retirement and aid the Rebel Alliance as a Jedi knight. He was once the teacher of Darth Vader.

Obi-Wan Kenobi, Luke Skywalker, and the two robots journey to the heavily guarded city of Mos Eisley. In Mos Eisley, a tough spaceport, they hope to find a pilot willing to make the hazardous trip to Alderaan. They soon find and hire Han Solo, captain of the spaceship *Millennium Falcon* and his first mate, the Wookie, Chewbacca.

16

The six fugitives get out of town just in time. They are closely followed by armed Imperial troops and destroyers, but manage to escape into hyperspace. On board, Obi-Wan Kenobi teaches Luke some more about being a Jedi knight. Artoo Detoo plays games with the Wookie.

Meanwhile in the Death Star, Darth Vader and Grand Moff Tarkin try without success to get information out of Princess Leia. In order to make her more cooperative, Darth forces her to watch as they blow up her home planet of Alderaan. The Princess is tough, however, and tosses off a lie to Darth. She describes the wrong location of the Rebel Alliance home base.

Imagine everyone's surprise when the *Millennium Falcon* comes out of hyperspace into an unexpected asteroid shower. In moments, there is a sickening silence as they realize that the asteroid shower is all that is left of Alderaan.

Before anyone knows what is happening, a tractor beam emerges from what seems to be a dark moon near the *Falcon.* The ship and its heroic crew are being drawn into the Death Star. There is no choice but to hide.

When the storm troopers board the *Falcon*, Luke and Han sneak up behind them and knock them out. Luke and Han change into the white armor of Imperial troopers, join Ben and Chewie and all sneak out of the ship to locate the Princess. Ben goes off to release the tractor beam so that the ship can leave again if possible.

The next few scenes involve high action familiar to adventure-story fans. The Princess is located, there is a laser pistol fight and escape from certain death in a garbage compactor. There are Tarzan-like swings across bottomless shafts, chase scenes, and a duel right out of *The Three Musketeers*. In this case, though, a hero dies in order to save the cause. Obi-Wan Kenobi allows himself to be cut down by Darth Vader, while everyone else runs to the ship and gets away in the confusion. Young Luke Skywalker is heartbroken to lose his friend and teacher, but with Kenobi's death, Luke realizes that he is now personally responsible for the success of the Rebels' mission. In the happy ending, the Death Star is destroyed, and Han Solo turns out to be a real friend.

Desert

Industrial Light and Magic Company is located in Van Nuys, California. But inside this company, John Dykstra, *Star War's* special effects wizard, creates sights and sounds for galaxies far, far away.

John Dykstra was trained in special effects by Doug Trumbull, another magician in the field. Trumbull created the effects for *2001: A Space Odyssey* and for *Close Encounters of the Third Kind.* Dykstra worked on Trumbull's crew in the science fiction film called *Silent Running.* In no time Dykstra learned to create fantastic effects. With *Star Wars,* Dykstra has become famous and has won an Oscar for his effects.

See-Threepio
and Artoo-Detoo

...the audience hang on
to their seats in alarm.

Because it is such a pleasure to just sit back and watch *Star Wars*, many people never realize that nearly every scene in the movie is the result of Dykstra's craft. A light saber looks so real that it is hard to imagine that the actors never fenced with anything more complicated than modified broom handles. The color and glow were added to the film long after the actors went home.

There are more special effects in *Star Wars*, and they are better than any other movie has ever made. In *Star Wars* special effects number 365, compared to 35 in *2001*. Industrial Light and Magic successfully creates illusions such as—a flight in space, a Jawa Sandcrawler, entrance into hyperspace, an exploding planet. And the effects are so well done that audiences see no faults even on a huge movie screen. When Luke Skywalker flies down the narrow channel of the Death Star to bomb it, the audience hang on to their seats in alarm.

The key to Dykstra's success is his attention to detail. All the small fighters in the *Millennium Falcon* and in the Death Star were tiny models made of spare parts from plastic kits purchased in toy stores. The rear of the *Falcon* was made with details from a model of a Sherman tank.

Nothing in *Star Wars* was meant to look new and out of place. After the models were built, they were painted to look used because in real life, things get pitted, dirty, and dented. Luke Skywalker's floating car had the right front grill bashed in, for example. After they were decorated, the tiny models were lighted from inside by tiny quartz lights. Then they were ready to be filmed.

Industrial Light and Magic also built large-scale models of the Sandcrawler, the *Falcon,* and the interiors of the Death Star. These models were extremely expensive because of the great detail needed to make them appear real.

The key to Dykstra's success is his attention to detail.

John Dykstra invented a camera that could move and photograph the models from any position. When he wanted to show a space ship flying, he moved the camera toward the model, rather than move the model around.

His camera can accurately accomplish these complex moves because it is computer controlled. The camera is called the Dykstraflex.

The Dykstraflex is mounted on a moving frame, and its computer can memorize the details of dives, swoops, rolls and other movements. And it can repeat any sequence exactly the same way time after time.

When Dykstra wanted to shoot a fight scene between two small craft, he used a procedure like this: He mounted the first ship on the model stand.

The camera dived toward the model at very slow speed, taking photos of the model at very high speed. This gave the illusion that the ship is moving very quickly.

Then he replaced the first ship with the second on the model stand. The computer told the camera to make the motions needed for this ship's flight. Then a photograph was taken of a large, black velvet screen covered with pin-prick holes. These holes were made in three sizes. When a bright light is focused at the back of the velvet, the front looks just like a starry night sky.

Dykstra then had his artists draw rods of light representing laser beams being fired back and forth. Finally, he put all of the pieces of film together into one print. The two ships were added, and the animated shots of light appeared to be streaming from one ship to the other.

These effects took a long time to produce. The effects for *Star Wars* were a full two years in the making, but ended up as the backbone for the whole movie.

Star Wars has many other illusions, too. All of the languages spoken by aliens are designed to sound like real speech. The Jawas speak a language that is part Zulu and part Swahili.

Greeto, the creature who picked the fight with Han Solo in the cantina, speaks a language based on ancient Incan. Even the Wookie, Chewbacca, makes expressive moans and roars.

Using real scenery is another important part of a film like *Star Wars*. This process is called "filming on location." Locations for this movie range from Tunisia to Death Valley. Tozeur is a town in an oasis in Southern Tunisia. It is located where Africa and Arabia meet and the Sahara Desert begins. This barren desert land became the planet Tatooine, where Luke Skywalker lived with his aunt and uncle.

Tozeur is an arid, dried-up wasteland dotted with an occasional palm tree. It is hot. Out in the desert dunes, the crew built the monster skeleton the robots' escape pod lands near at the beginning of the film. Another view of the area comes when Obi-Wan Kenobi, Luke and the two droids are looking down the cliff at Mos Eisley.

These effects took a long time to produce.

After shooting these scenes, the cast and crew moved to a town named Matmata. Matmata is inhabited by troglodytes. They are people who make their homes in caves cut in the sides of deep volcanic holes. These deep craters dot the landscape like craters on the Moon. Troglodytes live in their artificial caves for protection against the scorching sun of the summer and the bitter cold of the winter.

In Matmata, the Hotel Sidi Driss was taken over by the *Star Wars* bunch. The interior of the hotel became the inside of Luke's house when he and his aunt and uncle were eating together.

It was no simple task to make a movie in the desert. Heat strain hit the actor inside See Threepio, and motors kept breaking on Artoo Detoo. Sand seeped into cameras. Every night, the cameras had to be disassembled and cleaned. The film had to be kept in freezers so that it would not lose its strength.

Music is another important but unseen effect in *Star Wars*. The musical score was written by John Williams. Williams thought that the music should be traditional rather than electronic.

So he wrote a score which sounds very much like music written by late 19th-century Russian romantic composers. The march at the award ceremony at the end is heroic and stirring. The background music adds an exciting touch to every scene. Williams conducted the London Symphony Orchestra for the 90 minutes of music in *Star Wars*.

Droids

Star Wars begins with a conversation between its two most fascinating characters, Artoo Detoo and See Threepio. These two robots are widely praised as the best comedy team since Laurel and Hardy or Abbott and Costello. They are successful because George Lucas and his special-effects men worked very hard to make them real and appealing.

The golden droid, See Threepio, is a fussy worrier with excellent manners. He is a translating robot and can speak a thousand languages, including the beeps and whistles which Artoo Detoo uses. See Threepio is constantly afraid that his short friend will get them into some kind of mess for which they'll both be melted down.

Threepio's body appears to be made of solid gold plate, thanks to the magic of the *Star Wars* costume builders. However, it is actually made of steel, aluminum, fiberglass, plastic, and rubber. The whole body weighs 50 pounds—a heavy load for Anthony Daniels, the actor who made the robot come to life.

Daniels says that being inside the robot was the most painful experience of his life. The entire weight of the costume rested on his feet and on a neck strap. He couldn't walk more than a few steps without becoming too tired to go on.

See Threepio's heavy arms rested on Daniels' thumbs. His hands were numb for months at a time during filming. Every time Daniels moved, the costume would pinch him, cut him, or add another bruise. During filming on the desert, the temperature inside the costume would rise so much that Threepio resembled a walking sauna.

The costume was not designed so Daniels could sit down. During breaks, Daniels would have to be propped against a leaning board so that he could rest. He had to sip refreshments through a small straw. Since his arms didn't reach his mouth, someone would have to hold the cup to his mouth for him.

See Threepio is such a beautiful robot that members of the cast and crew were amazed the first time he appeared on the set. They soon got used to it, however, and some people even forgot that there was an actor inside the gold shell.

George Lucas didn't want a stiff, unnatural-looking robot in his movie. He selected Anthony Daniels, a 32-year-old mime, to play the part. Lucas felt that the graceful movements of a mime would help reduce the clumsiness of the Threepio costume. And whenever Threepio had to speak, Daniels could make some movement to help the audience locate the source of the sound.

George Lucas and his artist, Ralph McQuarrie, designed and rejected many masks before finding the right face for Threepio. They wanted a facial expression that would suit any emotion and would be interesting to view. The result was the very human and touching robot that often stole the show from his warm-blooded fellow actors.

Lenny Baker was more fortunate than Anthony Daniels. His costume as Artoo Detoo was quite comfortable. Baker, an actor and midget, could actually sit down inside the robot. And he only had to play Artoo Detoo when the robot was standing still, as when Luke was trying to get him to play back the tape from Princess Leia.

The R2 robot in the movie is actually seven different models. Some of these really were robots of sorts, and would roll and turn by remote control. Another model extended its arm to plug into the computer console on the Death Star.

Anthony Daniels often found himself confused when he would start a conversation with Artoo Detoo, only to find out that he was talking to a real robot and not to Kenny Baker.

Sound plays a very important part in *Star Wars*. Everything, even the noises of robots, had to sound exactly as George Lucas imagined it. Sound-effects man, Ben Burtt, and Lucas spent six months finding the exact right sounds for Artoo Detoo and See Threepio.

Lucas objected at first to the British accent of Anthony Daniels for the voice of See Threepio. He tried about thirty other voices of all kinds, and even tried synthesizing one. None of them was satisfactory. He returned to using Daniels' voice, but with a slight electronic distortion. The formal, fussy voice matches the character of See Threepio perfectly.

Artoo Detoo's language problem was much harder to solve. Burtt and Lucas were so painstaking in designing this robot's voice that what seem to be random whistles and sighs are actually sounds like real English.

All of these details and more went into the success forumla for See Threepio and Artoo Detoo. This duo will be remembered for a long time and will be welcome old friends in every *Star Wars* sequel.